Bridget Woodcock.

A FEW
LATE CHRYSANTHEMUMS

A FEW LATE CHRYSANTHEMUMS

*

BY

JOHN BETJEMAN

LONDON

JOHN MURRAY, ALBEMARLE STREET

By the same author

Poems

SELECTED POEMS

Prose

FIRST AND LAST LOVES

First Edition   July 1954
Reprinted   January 1955
Reprinted November 1955

Made and printed in Great Britain by
William Clowes and Sons, Limited, London and Beccles

Contents

*

MEDIUM

*

GLOOM

*

CONTENTS

LIGHT

*

Acknowledgements

I have to thank the Editors of *The Times Literary Supplement*, *The Harrovian*, *The New Statesman*, *The Cornhill*, *Punch*, *Tribune*, *Time and Tide*, *The Observer*, *Harper's Bazaar*, *Harlequin* and *The Saturday Book* for permission to reprint these poems. Also I should like to thank Mr. John Sparrow for some sensitive and wise corrections to several of the poems.

For Elizabeth

MEDIUM

Sunday Morning King's Cambridge

FILE into yellow candle light, fair choristers of
King's
Lost in the shadowy silence of canopied
Renaissance stalls
In blazing glass above the dark glow skies and
thrones and wings
Blue, ruby, gold and green between the
whiteness of the walls
And with what rich precision the stonework
soars and springs
To fountain out a spreading vault— a shower
that never falls.

The white of windy Cambridge courts, the
cobbles brown and dry,
The gold of plaster Gothic with ivy over-
grown,
The apple-red, the silver fronts, the wide green
flats and high,

3

The yellowing elm-trees circled out on islands
of their own—
Oh, here behold all colours change that catch
the flying sky
To waves of pearly light that heave along the
shafted stone.

In far East Anglian churches, the clasped hands
lying long
Recumbent on sepulchral slabs or effigied in
brass
Buttress with prayer this vaulted roof so white
and light and strong
And countless congregations as the genera-
tions pass
Join choir and great crowned organ case, in
centuries of song
To praise Eternity contained in Time and
coloured glass.

4

Harrow-on-the-Hill

WHEN melancholy Autumn comes to Wembley
  And electric trains are lighted after tea
The poplars near the Stadium are trembly
  With their tap and tap and whispering to me,
      Like the sound of little breakers
      Spreading out along the surf-line
When the estuary's filling
      With the sea.

Then Harrow-on-the-Hill's a rocky island
  And Harrow churchyard full of sailors' graves
And the constant click and kissing of the trolley
      buses hissing
  Is the level to the Wealdstone turned to waves
      And the rumble of the railway
      Is the thunder of the rollers
As they gather up for plunging
      Into caves.

There's a storm cloud to the westward over
 Kenton,
   There's a line of harbour lights at Perivale,
Is it rounding rough Pentire in a flood of sunset
 fire
   The little fleet of trawlers under sail ?
     Can those boats be only roof tops
     As they stream along the skyline
In a race for port and Padstow
     With the gale ?

*Verses turned
in aid of A Public Subscription (1952)
Towards the restoration of the
Church of St. Katherine
Chiselhampton, Oxon*

Across the wet November night

The church is bright with candlelight

    And waiting Evensong.

A single bell with plaintive strokes

Pleads louder than the stirring oaks

    The leafless lanes along.

It calls the choirboys from their tea

And villagers, the two or three,

    Damp down the kitchen fire,

Let out the cat, and up the lane

Go paddling through the gentle rain

    Of misty Oxfordshire.

How warm the many candles shine
On SAMUEL DOWBIGGIN's design
   For this interior neat,
These high box pews of Georgian days
Which screen us from the public gaze
   When we make answer meet ;

How gracefully their shadow falls
On bold pilasters down the walls
   And on the pulpit high.
The chandeliers would twinkle gold
As pre-Tractarian sermons roll'd
   Doctrinal, sound and dry.

From that west gallery no doubt
The viol and serpent tooted out
   The Tallis tune to Ken,
And firmly at the end of prayers
The clerk below the pulpit stairs
   Would thunder out " Amen."

But every wand'ring thought will cease
Before the noble altarpiece
   With carven swags array'd,
For there in letters all may read
The Lord's Commandments, Prayer and
      Creed,
   And decently display'd.

On country mornings sharp and clear
The penitent in faith draw near
   And kneeling here below
Partake the Heavenly Banquet spread
Of Sacramental Wine and Bread
   And JESUS' presence know.

And must that plaintive bell in vain
Plead loud along the dripping lane ?
   And must the building fall ?
Not while we love the Church and live
And of our charity will give
   Our much, our more, our all.

Christmas

THE bells of waiting Advent ring,
  The Tortoise stove is lit again
And lamp-oil light across the night
  Has caught the streaks of winter rain
In many a stained-glass window sheen
From Crimson Lake to Hooker's Green.

The holly in the windy hedge
  And round the Manor House the yew
Will soon be stripped to deck the ledge,
  The altar, font and arch and pew,
So that the villagers can say
" The church looks nice " on Christmas Day.

Provincial public houses blaze
  And Corporation tramcars clang,
On lighted tenements I gaze
  Where paper decorations hang,
And bunting in the red Town Hall
Says " Merry Christmas to you all. '

CHRISTMAS

And London shops on Christmas Eve
   Are strung with silver bells and flowers
As hurrying clerks the City leave
   To pigeon-haunted classic towers,
And marbled clouds go scudding by
The many-steepled London sky.

And girls in slacks remember Dad,
   And oafish louts remember Mum,
And sleepless children's hearts are glad,
   And Christmas-morning bells say " Come ! "
Even to shining ones who dwell
Safe in the Dorchester Hotel.

And is it true ? And is it true,
   This most tremendous tale of all,
Seen in a stained-glass window's hue,
   A Baby in an ox's stall ?
The Maker of the stars and sea
Become a Child on earth for me ?

CHRISTMAS

And is it true ?   For if it is,
   No loving fingers tying strings
Around those tissued fripperies,
   The sweet and silly Christmas things,
Bath salts and inexpensive scent
And hideous tie so kindly meant,

No love that in a family dwells,
   No carolling in frosty air,
Nor all the steeple-shaking bells
   Can with this single Truth compare—
That God was Man in Palestine
And lives to-day in Bread and Wine.

The Licorice Fields at Pontefract

In the licorice fields at Pontefract
   My love and I did meet
And many a burdened licorice bush
   Was blooming round our feet;
Red hair she had and golden skin,
Her sulky lips were shaped for sin,
Her sturdy legs were flannel-slack'd.
The strongest legs in Pontefract.

The light and dangling licorice flowers
   Gave off the sweetest smells ;
From various black Victorian towers
   The Sunday evening bells
Came pealing over dales and hills
And tanneries and silent mills
And lowly streets where country stops
And little shuttered corner shops.

13

THE LICORICE FIELDS AT PONTEFRACT

She cast her blazing eyes on me
    And plucked a licorice leaf;
I was her captive slave and she
    My red-haired robber chief.
Oh love ! for love I could not speak,
It left me winded, wilting, weak
And held in brown arms strong and bare
And wound with flaming ropes of hair.

Church of England thoughts occa-
sioned by hearing the bells of Mag-
dalen Tower from the Botanic Garden
Oxford on St. Mary Magdalen's Day

I SEE the urn against the yew,

    The sunlit urn of sculptured stone,

I see its shapely shadow fall

On this enormous garden wall

    Which makes a kingdom of its own :

A grassy kingdom sweet to view

    With tiger lilies still in flower

And beds of umbelliferæ

Ranged in Linnaean symmetry,

    All in the sound of Magdalen tower.

A multiplicity of bells,

    A changing cadence, rich and deep

Swung from those pinnacles on high

To fill the trees and flood the sky

    And rock the sailing clouds to sleep.

15

CHURCH OF ENGLAND THOUGHTS

A Church of England sound, it tells
　　Of " moderate " worship, God and State,
Where mattins congregations go
Conservative and good and slow
　　To elevations of the plate.

And loud through resin-scented chines
　　And purple rhododendrons roll'd,
I hear the bells for Eucharist
From churches blue with incense mist
　　Where reredoses twinkle gold.

Chapels-of-ease by railway lines
　　And humble streets and smells of gas !
I hear your plaintive ting-tangs call
From many a gabled western wall
　　To Morning Prayer or Holy Mass.

In country churches old and pale
　　I hear the changes smoothly rung
And watch the coloured sallies fly
From rugged hands to rafters high
　　As round and back the bells are swung.

16

CHURCH OF ENGLAND THOUGHTS

Before the spell begin to fail,
    Before the bells have lost their power,
Before the grassy kingdom fade
And Oxford traffic roar invade,
    I thank the bells of Magdalen Tower.

Essex

" THE vagrant visitor erstwhile,"
  My colour-plate book says to me,
" Could wend by hedgerow-side and stile,
  From Benfleet down to Leigh-on-Sea."

And as I turn the colour-plates
  Edwardian Essex opens wide,
Mirrored in ponds and seen through gates,
  Sweet uneventful countryside.

Like streams the little by-roads run
  Through oats and barley round a hill
To where blue willows catch the sun
  By some white weather-boarded mill.

" A Summer Idyll Matching Tye "
  " At Havering-atte-Bower, the Stocks "
And cobbled pathways lead the eye
  To cottage doors and hollyhocks.

18

ESSEX

Far Essex,—fifty miles away
  The level wastes of sucking mud
Where distant barges high with hay
  Come sailing in upon the flood.

Near Essex of the River Lea
  And anglers out with hook and worm
And Epping Forest glades where we
  Had beanfeasts with my father's firm.

At huge and convoluted pubs
  They used to set us down from brakes
In that half-land of football clubs
  Which London near the Forest makes.

Then deepest Essex few explore
  Where steepest thatch is sunk in flowers
And out of elm and sycamore
  Rise flinty fifteenth-century towers.

ESSEX

I see the little branch line go
    By white farms roofed in red and brown,
The old Great Eastern winding slow
    To some forgotten country town.

Now yarrow chokes the railway track,
    Brambles obliterate the stile,
No motor coach can take me back
    To that Edwardian " erstwhile."

Huxley Hall

In the Garden City Café with its murals on the
    wall
Before a talk on " Sex and Civics " I meditated
    on the Fall.

Deep depression settled on me under that
    electric glare
While outside the lightsome poplars flanked
    the rose-beds in the square.

While outside the carefree children sported in
    the summer haze
And released their inhibitions in a hundred
    different ways.

She who eats her greasy crumpets snugly in the
    inglenook
Of some birch-enshrouded homestead, dropping
    butter on her book,

21

HUXLEY HALL

Can she know the deep depression of this bright,
    hygienic hell ?
And her husband, stout free-thinker, can he
    share in it as well ?

Not the folk-museum's charting of man's Pro-
    gress out of slime
Can release me from the painful seeming
    accident of Time.

Barry smashes Shirley's dolly, Shirley's eyes
    are crossed with hate,
Comrades plot a Comrade's downfall "in the
    interests of the State."

Not my vegetarian dinner, not my lime-juice
    minus gin,
Quite can drown a faint conviction that we
    may be born in Sin.

House of Rest

Now all the world she knew is dead
    In this small room she lives her days,
The wash-hand stand and single bed
    Screened from the public gaze.

The horse-brass shines, the kettle sings,
    The cup of China tea
Is tasted among cared-for things
    Ranged round for me to see—

Lincoln, by Valentine and Co.,
    Now yellowish brown and stained,
But there some fifty years ago
    Her Harry was ordained ;

Outside the Church at Woodhall Spa
    The smiling groom and bride,
And here's his old tobacco jar
    Dried lavender inside.

HOUSE OF REST

I do not like to ask if he
  Was " High " or " Low " or " Broad "
Lest such a question seem to be
  A mockery of Our Lord.

Her full grey eyes look far beyond
  The little room and me
To village church and village pond
  And ample rectory.

She sees her children each in place
  Eyes downcast as they wait,
She hears her Harry murmur Grace,
  Then heaps the porridge plate.

Aroused at seven, to bed by ten,
  They fully lived each day,
Dead sons, so motor-bike-mad then,
  And daughters far away.

24

HOUSE OF REST

Now when the bells for Eucharist
  Sound in the Market Square,
With sunshine struggling through the mist
  And Sunday in the air,

The veil between her and her dead
  Dissolves and shows them clear,
The Consecration Prayer is said
  And all of them are near.

Middlesex

GAILY into Ruislip Gardens
    Runs the red electric train,
With a thousand Ta's and Pardon's
    Daintily alights Elaine ;
Hurries down the concrete station
With a frown of concentration,
Out into the outskirt's edges
Where a few surviving hedges
Keep alive our lost Elysium—rural Middlesex
    again.

Well cut Windsmoor flapping lightly,
    Jacqmar scarf of mauve and green
Hiding hair which, Friday nightly,
    Delicately drowns in Drene ;
Fair Elaine the bobby-soxer,
Fresh-complexioned with Innoxa,
Gains the garden—father's hobby—
Hangs her Windsmoor in the lobby,
Settles down to sandwich supper and the tele-
    vision screen.

MIDDLESEX

Gentle Brent, I used to know you
    Wandering Wembley-wards at will,
Now what change your waters show you
    In the meadowlands you fill !
Recollect the elm-trees misty
And the footpaths climbing twisty
Under cedar-shaded palings,
Low laburnum-leaned-on railings,
Out of Northolt on and upward to the heights
    of Harrow hill.

Parish of enormous hayfields
    Perivale stood all alone,
And from Greenford scent of mayfields
    Most enticingly was blown
Over market gardens tidy,
Taverns for the *bona fide*,
Cockney anglers, cockney shooters,
Murray Poshes, Lupin Pooters
Long in Kensal Green and Highgate silent under
    soot and stone.

Seaside Golf

How straight it flew, how long it flew,
   It clear'd the rutty track
And soaring, disappeared from view
   Beyond the bunker's back—
A glorious, sailing, bounding drive
That made me glad I was alive.

And down the fairway, far along
   It glowed a lonely white ;
I played an iron sure and strong
   And clipp'd it out of sight,
And spite of grassy banks between
I knew I'd find it on the green.

And so I did.   It lay content
   Two paces from the pin;
A steady putt and then it went
   Oh, most securely in.
The very turf rejoiced to see
That quite unprecedented three.

SEASIDE GOLF

Ah ! seaweed smells from sandy caves
    And thyme and mist in whiffs,
In-coming tide, Atlantic waves
    Slapping the sunny cliffs,
Lark song and sea sounds in the air
And splendour, splendour everywhere.

GLOOM

I.M.
Walter Ramsden
ob. March 26 1947
Pembroke College, Oxford

DR. RAMSDEN cannot read *The Times* obituary
>   to-day,
> He's dead.
Let monographs on silk worms by other people
>   be
> Thrown away
> Unread
For he who best could understand and criticize
>   them, he
> Lies clay
> In bed.

The body waits in Pembroke College
Where the ivy taps the panes
> All night;
That old head so full of knowledge,

I.M. WALTER RAMSDEN

That good heart that kept the brains
    All right,
Those old cheeks that faintly flushed as the port
      suffused the veins,
    Drain'd white.

Crocus in the Fellows' Garden, winter jasmine
      up the wall
    Gleam gold.
Shadows of Victorian chimneys on the sunny
      grassplot fall
    Long, cold.
Master, Bursar, Senior Tutor, these, his three
      survivors, all
    Feel old.

They remember, as the coffin to its final obse-
      quations
    Leaves the gates,
Buzz of bees in window boxes on their summer
      ministrations,
    Kitchen din,

I.M. WALTER RAMSDEN

Cups and plates,
And the getting of bump suppers for the long
    dead generations
Coming in,
From Eights.

Norfolk

How did the Devil come ? When first attack ?
  These Norfolk lanes recall lost innocence,
The years fall off and find me walking back
  Dragging a stick along the wooden fence
Down this same path, where, forty years ago,
My father strolled behind me, calm and slow.

I used to fill my hand with sorrel seeds
  And shower him with them from the tops of
    stiles,
I used to butt my head into his tweeds
  To make him hurry down those languorous
    miles
Of ash and alder-shaded lanes, till here
Our moorings and the masthead would appear.

There after supper lit by lantern light
  Warm in the cabin I could lie secure
And hear against the polished sides at night

36

NORFOLK

The lap lap lapping of the weedy Bure,
A whispering and watery Norfolk sound
Telling of all the moonlit reeds around.

How did the Devil come ?   When first attack ?
  The church is just the same, though now I
    know
Fowler of Louth restored it.   Time, bring back
  The rapturous ignorance of long ago,
The peace, before the dreadful daylight starts,
Of unkept promises and broken hearts.

The Metropolitan Railway

BAKER STREET STATION BUFFET

EARLY Electric !   With what radiant hope
   Men formed this many-branched electrolier,
Twisted the flex around the iron rope
   And let the dazzling vacuum globes hang
      clear,
And then with hearts the rich contrivance fill'd
Of copper, beaten by the Bromsgrove Guild.

Early Electric !   Sit you down and see,
   'Mid this fine woodwork and a smell of dinner,
A stained-glass windmill and a pot of tea,
   And sepia views of leafy lanes in PINNER,—
Then visualise, far down the shining lines,
Your parents' homestead set in murmuring
      pines.

THE METROPOLITAN RAILWAY

Smoothly from HARROW, passing PRESTON
    ROAD,
  They saw the last green fields and misty sky,
At NEASDEN watched a workmen's train unload,
  And, with the morning villas sliding by,
They felt so sure on their electric trip
That Youth and Progress were in partnership.

And all that day in murky London Wall
  The thought of RUISLIP kept him warm
    inside ;
At FARRINGDON that lunch hour at a stall
  He bought a dozen plants of London Pride ;
While she, in arc-lit Oxford Street adrift,
Soared through the sales by safe hydraulic
    lift.

Early Electric ! Maybe even here
  They met that evening at six-fifteen
Beneath the hearts of this electrolier

And caught the first non-stop to WILLESDEN
    GREEN,
Then out and on, through rural RAYNER'S LANE
To autumn-scented Middlesex again.

Cancer has killed him.   Heart is killing her.
    The trees are down.   An Odeon flashes fire
Where stood their villa by the murmuring fir
    When " they would for their children's good
        conspire."
Of all their loves and hopes on hurrying feet
Thou art the worn memorial, Baker Street.

Late-Flowering Lust

My head is bald, my breath is bad,
    Unshaven is my chin,
I have not now the joys I had
    When I was young in sin.

I run my fingers down your dress
    With brandy-certain aim
And you respond to my caress
    And maybe feel the same.

But I've a picture of my own
    On this reunion night,
Wherein two skeletons are shewn
    To hold each other tight;

Dark sockets look on emptiness
    Which once was loving-eyed,
The mouth that opens for a kiss
    Has got no tongue inside.

LATE-FLOWERING LUST

I cling to you inflamed with fear
    As now you cling to me,
I feel how frail you are my dear
    And wonder what will be—

A week ? or twenty years remain ?
    And then—what kind of death ?
A losing fight with frightful pain
    Or a gasping fight for breath ?

Too long we let our bodies cling,
    We cannot hide disgust
At all the thoughts that in us spring
    From this late-flowering lust.

Sun and Fun
SONG OF A NIGHT-CLUB PROPRIETRESS

I WALKED into the night-club in the morning,
   There was kummel on the handle of the door,
The ashtrays were unemptied,
The cleaning unattempted,
   And a squashed tomato sandwich on the floor.

I pulled aside the thick magenta curtains
   —So Regency, so Regency, my dear—
And a host of little spiders
Ran a race across the ciders
   To a box of baby 'pollies by the beer.

Oh sun upon the summer-going by-pass
   Where ev'rything is speeding to the sea,
And wonder beyond wonder
That here where lorries thunder
   The sun should ever percolate to me.

43

SUN AND FUN

When Boris used to call in his Sedanca,
    When Teddy took me down to his estate,
When my nose excited passion,
When my clothes were in the fashion,
    When my beaux were never cross if I was late,

There was sun enough for lazing upon beaches,
    There was fun enough for far into the night.
But I'm dying now and done for,
What on earth was all the fun for ?
    For God's sake keep that sunlight out of sight.

Original Sin on the Sussex Coast

Now on this out of season afternoon
Day schools which cater for the sort of boy
Whose parents go by Pullman once a month
To do a show in town, pour out their young
Into the sharply red October light.
Here where The Drive and Buckhurst Road
    converge
I watch the rival gangs and am myself
A schoolboy once again in shivering shorts.
I see the dust of sherbet on the chin
Of Andrew Knox well-dress'd, well-born, well-
    fed,
Even at nine a perfect gentleman,
Willie Buchanan waiting at his side
Another Scot, eruptions on his skin.
I hear Jack Drayton whistling from the fence
Which hides the copper domes of " Cooch
    Behar."
That was the signal.   So there's no escape.
A race for Willow Way and jump the hedge

Behind the Granville Bowling Club ?   Too late.

They'll catch me coming out in Seapink Lane.

Across the Garden of Remembrance ?   No,

That would be blasphemy and bring bad luck.

Well then, I'm *for* it.   Andrew's at me first,

He pinions me in that especial grip

His brother learned in Kobë from a Jap

(No chance for me against the Japanese).

Willie arrives and winds me with a punch

Plum in the tummy, grips the other arm.

" You're to be booted. Hold him steady
    chaps ! "

A wait for taking aim.   Oh trees and sky !

Then crack against the column of my spine,

Blackness and breathlessness and sick with pain

I stumble on the asphalt.   Off they go

Away, away, thank God, and out of sight

So that I lie quite still and climb to sense

Too out of breath and strength to make a sound.

   Now over Polegate vastly sets the sun;

Dark rise the Downs from darker looking elms,

And out of Southern railway trains to tea

ORIGINAL SIN ON THE SUSSEX COAST

Run happy boys down various Station Roads,
Satchels of homework jogging on their backs,
So trivial and so healthy in the shade
Of these enormous Downs.   And when they're
     home,
When the Post-Toasties mixed with Golden
     Shred
Make for the kiddies such a scrumptious feast,
Does Mum, the Persil-user, still believe
That there's no Devil and that youth is bliss ?
As certain as the sun behind the Downs
And quite as plain to see, the Devil walks.

Devonshire Street W.1

THE heavy mahogany door with its wrought-
  iron screen
  Shuts. And the sound is rich, sympathetic,
  discreet.
The sun still shines on this eighteenth-century
  scene
  With Edwardian faience adornments —
  Devonshire Street.

No hope. And the X-ray photographs under
  his arm
  Confirm the message. His wife stands
  timidly by.
The opposite brick-built house looks lofty and
  calm
  Its chimneys steady against a mackerel sky.

DEVONSHIRE STREET W.1.

No hope. And the iron nob of this palisade
  So cold to the touch, is luckier now than he
" Oh merciless, hurrying Londoners ! Why
    was I made
  For the long and the painful deathbed coming
    to me ? "

She puts her fingers in his as, loving and silly,
  At long-past Kensington dances she used
    to do
" It's cheaper to take the tube to Piccadilly
  And then we can catch a nineteen or a
    twenty-two."

The Cottage Hospital

AT the end of a long-walled garden
    in a red provincial town,
A brick path led to a mulberry
    scanty grass at its feet.
I lay under blackening branches
    where the mulberry leaves hung down
Sheltering ruby fruit globes
    from a Sunday-tea-time heat.
Apple and plum espaliers
    basked upon bricks of brown;
The air was swimming with insects,
    and children played in the street.

Out of this bright intentness
    into the mulberry shade
Musca domestica (housefly)
    swung from the August light
Slap into slithery rigging
    by the waiting spider made

THE COTTAGE HOSPITAL

Which spun the lithe elastic
   till the fly was shrouded tight.
Down came the hairy talons
   and horrible poison blade
And none of the garden noticed
   that fizzing, hopeless fight.

Say in what Cottage Hospital
   whose pale green walls resound
With the tap upon polished parquet
   of inflexible nurses' feet
Shall I myself be lying
   when they range the screens around ?
And say shall I groan in dying,
   as I twist the sweaty sheet ?
Or gasp for breath uncrying,
   as I feel my senses drown'd
While the air is swimming with insects
   and children play in the street.

A Child Ill

Oh, little body, do not die.
  The soul looks out through wide blue eyes
So questioningly into mine,
  That my tormented soul replies :
" Oh, little body, do not die.
  You hold the soul that talks to me
Although our conversation be
  As wordless as the windy sky."

So looked my father at the last
  Right in my soul, before he died,
Though words we spoke went heedless
      past
  As London traffic-roar outside.
And now the same blue eyes I see
  Look through me from a little son,
So questioning, so searchingly
  That youthfulness and age are one.

52

A CHILD ILL

My father looked at me and died
Before my soul made full reply.
Lord, leave this other Light alight—
Oh, little body, do not die.

Variation on a Theme by
T. W. Rolleston

UNDER the ground, on a Saturday afternoon in
 winter
 Lies a mother of five,
And frost has bitten the purple November rose
 flowers
 Which budded when *she* was alive.

They have switched on the street lamps here
 by the cemet'ry railing;
 In the dying afternoon
Men from football, and women from Timothy
 White's and McIlroy's
 Will be coming teawards soon.

But her place is empty in the queue at the Inter-
 national,
 The greengrocer's queue lacks one,
So does the crowd at Mac Fisheries. There's no
 one to go to Freeman's
 To ask if the shoes are done.

VARIATION ON A THEME

Will she, who was so particular, be glad to know
    that after
  The tears, the prayers and the priest,
Her clothing coupons and ration book were
    handed in at the Food Office
  For the files marked " deceased " ?

Business Girls

FROM the geyser ventilators
    Autumn winds are blowing down
On a thousand business women
    Having baths in Camden Town.

Waste pipes chuckle into runnels,
    Steam's escaping here and there,
Morning trains through Camden cutting
    Shake the Crescent and the Square.

Early nip of changeful autumn,
    Dahlias glimpsed through garden doors,
At the back precarious bathrooms
    Jutting out from upper floors,

BUSINESS GIRLS

And behind their frail partitions
   Business women lie and soak,
Seeing through the draughty skylight
   Flying clouds and railway smoke.

Rest you there, poor unbelov'd ones,
   Lap your loneliness in heat.
All too soon the tiny breakfast,
   Trolley-bus and windy street !

Remorse

The lungs draw in the air and rattle it out again;
　The eyes revolve in their sockets and upwards
　　stare ;
No more worry and waiting and troublesome
　　doubt again—
　She whom I loved and left is no longer there.

The nurse lays down her knitting and walks
　　across to her
　With quick professional eye she surveys the
　　dead.
Just one patient the less and little the loss to her,
　Distantly tender she settles the shrunken
　　head.

Protestant claims and Catholic, the wrong and
　　the right of them,
　Unimportant they seem in the face of death—

58

But my neglect and unkindness—to lose the
    sight of them
  I would listen even again to that labouring
    breath.

The Old Liberals

PALE green of the *English Hymnal*!   Yattendon
   hymns
    Played on the *hautbois* by a lady dress'd in
    blue
    Her white-hair'd father accompanying her
    thereto
On tenor or bass-recorder.   Daylight swims
   On sectional bookcase, delicate cup and plate
   And William de Morgan tiles around the grate
And many the silver birches the pearly light
   shines through.

I think such a running together of woodwind
   sound,
   Such painstaking piping high on a Berkshire
   hill,
   Is sad as an English autumn heavy and still,
Sad as a country silence, tractor-drowned;
For deep in the hearts of the man and the
   woman playing

THE OLD LIBERALS

The rose of a world that was not has withered
away.
Where are the wains with garlanded swathes
a-swaying ?
Where are the swains to wend through the lanes
a-maying ?
Where are the blithe and jocund to ted the
hay ?
Where are the free folk of England ?   Where
are they ?

Ask of the Abingdon bus with full load creeping
Down into denser suburbs.   The birch lets go
But one brown leaf upon browner bracken
below.
Ask of the cinema manager.   Night airs die
To still, ripe scent of the fungus and wet woods
weeping.
Ask at the fish and chips in the Market Square.
Here amid firs and a final sunset flare
Recorder and *hautbois* only moan at a moulder-
ing sky.

61

Clay and Spirit

Yellow November flowering ivy,
   Penned-up sheep and the stacked-up hay,
Crested gold over purple scrubland
   Elm trees rot in a still decay.

Water rushes through limestone arches
   Whirls the leaves a parish away,
" One, two, three," in a fungus odour,
   The bellcote summons for All Saints' Day

" One, two, three," to a cold stone chancel,
   Two small lights and a priest to pray ;
Humming machines on a misty landscape
   Drown the sound of the soaking clay.

CLAY AND SPIRIT

Out of the clay the Saints were moulded,
    Out of the clay the Wine and Bread,
But out of the Soul the heart that withers,
    As brains increase in the big white head.

Greenaway

I know so well this turfy mile,
    These clumps of sea-pink withered brown,
The breezy cliff, the awkward stile,
    The sandy path that takes me down

To crackling layers of broken slate
    Where black and flat sea-woodlice crawl
And isolated rock pools wait
    Wash from the highest tides of all.

I know the roughly blasted track
    That skirts a small and smelly bay
And over squelching bladderwrack
    Leads to the beach at Greenaway.

Down on the shingle safe at last
    I hear the slowly dragging roar
As mighty rollers mount to cast
    Small coal and seaweed on the shore,

And spurting far as it can reach
　The shooting surf comes hissing round
To leave a line along the beach
　Of cowries waiting to be found.

Tide after tide by night and day
　The breakers battle with the land
And rounded smooth along the bay
　The faithful rocks protecting stand.

But in a dream the other night
　I saw this coastline from the sea
And felt the breakers plunging white
　Their weight of waters over me.

There were the stile, the turf, the shore,
　The safety line of shingle beach
With every stroke I struck the more
　The backwash sucked me out of reach.

GREENAWAY

Back into what a water-world
    Of waving weed and waiting claws ?
Of writhing tentacles uncurled
    To drag me to what dreadful jaws ?

LIGHT

The Olympic Girl

THE sort of girl I like to see
Smiles down from her great height at me.
She stands in strong, athletic pose
And wrinkles her *retroussé* nose.
Is it distaste that makes her frown,
So furious and freckled, down
On an unhealthy worm like me ?
Or am I what she likes to see ?
I do not know, though much I care.
εἶθε γενοίμην   . . . would I were
(Forgive me, shade of Rupert Brooke)
An object fit to claim her look.
Oh ! would I were her racket press'd
With hard excitement to her breast
And swished into the sunlit air
Arm-high above her tousled hair,
And banged against the bounding ball
" Oh !   Plung ! " my tauten'd strings would
    call,
" Oh !   Plung ! my darling, break my strings

69

THE OLYMPIC GIRL

For you I will do brilliant things."
And when the match is over, I
Would flop beside you, hear you sigh ;
And then, with what supreme caress,
You'ld tuck me up into my press.
Fair tigress of the tennis courts,
So short in sleeve and strong in shorts,
Little, alas, to you I mean,
For I am bald and old and green.

The Weary Journalist

HERE, on this far North London height
I sit and write and write and write;
I pull the nothings from my head
And weight them round with lumps of lead
Then plonk them down upon the page
In finely simulated rage.

Whither Democracy ?   I ask
And What the Nature of her Task ?
Whither Bulgaria and Peru ?
What Crisis are they passing through ?
Before my readers can reply
Essential Factors flutter by,
Parlous, indeed, is their condition
Until they find a Key Position.
To keep their Tendencies in Check
I push them through a Bottleneck
From which they Challenge me and frown
And Fling their Tattered Gauntlets down
And Vital Problems sit and trill
Outside upon my window sill

THE WEARY JOURNALIST

And Lies are wrapped around in Tissues
And oh ! the crowds of Vital Issues.
I ache in all my mental joints
Nigh stabbed to death by Focal Points.
But all the time I know, I know
That ev'ry twinkling light below
Shines on a Worker in his Vest
(True symbol of the Great Oppress'd)
And he, like all unheeding fools,
Is filling in his football pools.

The Dear Old Village

THE dear old village ! *Lin-lan-lone* the bells
(Which should be six) ring over hills and dells,
But since the row about the ringers' tea
It's *lin-lan-lone*.   They're only ringing three.
The elm leaves patter like a summer shower
As *lin-lan-lone* pours through them from the
     tower.
From that embattled, lichen-crusted fane
Which scoops the sun into each western pane,
The bells ring over hills and dells in vain.
For we are free to-day.   No need to praise
The Unseen Author of our nights and days;
No need to hymn the rich uncurling spring
For DYKES is nowhere half so good as BING.
Nature is out of date and GOD is too;
Think what atomic energy can do !

  Farmers have wired the public rights-of-way
Should any wish to walk to church to pray.
Along the village street the sunset strikes
On young men tuning up their motor-bikes,

And country girls with lips and nails vermilion
Wait, nylon-legged, to straddle on the pillion.
Off to the roadhouse and the Tudor Bar
And then the Sunday-opened cinema.
While to the church's iron-studded door
Go two old ladies and a child of four.

    This is the age of progress.   Let us meet
The new progressives of the village street.
Hear not the water lapsing down the rills,
Lift not your eyes to the surrounding hills,
While spring recalls the miracle of birth
Let us, for heaven's sake, keep down to earth.

    See that square house, late Georgian and
      smart,
Two fields away it proudly stands apart,
Dutch barn and concrete cow-sheds have re-
      placed
The old thatched roofs which once the yard dis-
      graced.
Here wallows Farmer WHISTLE in his riches,
His ample stomach heaved above his breeches.
You'd never think that in such honest beef
Lurk'd an adulterous braggart, liar and thief.

His wife brought with her thirty-thousand
 down :
He keeps his doxy in the nearest town.
No man more anxious on the R.D.C.
For better rural cottages than he,
Especially when he had some land to sell
Which, as a site, would suit the Council well.
So three times what he gave for it he got,
For one undrainable and useless plot
Where now the hideous Council houses stand.
Unworked on and unworkable their land,
The wind blows under each unseason'd door,
The floods pour over every kitchen floor,
And country wit, which likes to laugh at sin,
Christens the Council houses " Whistle's Win."
Woe to some lesser farmer who may try
To call his bluff or to expose his lie.
Remorseless as a shark in London's City,
He gets at them through the War Ag. Com-
 mittee.

 He takes no part in village life beyond
Throwing his refuse in a neighbour's pond
And closing footpaths, not repairing walls,

Leaving a cottage till at last it falls.

People protest.   A law-suit then begins,

But as he's on the Bench, he always wins.

   Behind rank elders, shadowing a pool,

And near the Church, behold the Village School,

Its gable rising out of ivy thick

Shows " Eighteen-Sixty " worked in coloured
     brick.

By nineteen-forty-seven, hurrah ! hooray !

This institution has outlived its day.

In the bad times of old feudality

The villagers were ruled by masters three—

Squire, parson, schoolmaster.   Of these, the last

Knew best the village present and its past.

Now, I am glad to say, the man is dead,

The children have a motor-bus instead,

And in a town eleven miles away

We train them to be " Citizens of To-day."

And many a cultivated hour they pass

In a fine school with walls of vita-glass.

Civics, eurhythmics, economics, Marx,

How-to-respect-wild-life-in-National-Parks ;

Plastics, gymnastics—thus they learn to scorn

THE DEAR OLD VILLAGE

The old thatch'd cottages where they were born.
The girls, ambitious to begin their lives
Serving in WOOLWORTH'S, rather than as wives ;
The boys, who cannot yet escape the land,
At driving tractors lend a clumsy hand.
An eight-hour day for all, and more than three
Of these are occupied in making tea
And talking over what we all agree—
Though " Music while you work " is now our
    wont,
It's not so nice as " Music while you don't."
Squire, parson, schoolmaster turn in their
    graves.
And *let* them turn. We are no longer slaves.

  So much for youth. I fear we older folk
Must be dash'd off with a more hurried stroke.
Old Mrs. SPEAK has cut, for fifteen years,
Her husband's widowed sister Mrs. SHEARS,
Though how she's managed it, I cannot say,
Sharing a cottage with her night and day.
What caused the quarrel fifteen years ago
And how BERT SPEAK gets on, I do not know,
There the three live in that old dwelling quaint

77

THE DEAR OLD VILLAGE

Which water-colourists delight to paint.

Of the large brood round Mrs. COKER's door,

Coker has definitely fathered four

And two are Farmer Whistle's : two they say

Have coloured fathers in the U.S.A.

I learn'd all this and more from Mrs. FREE,

Pride of the Women's Institute is she,

Says " Sir " or " Madam " to you, knows her
    station

And how to make a quiet insinuation.

The unrespectable must well know why

They fear her lantern jaw and leaden eye.

  There is no space to tell about the chaps—

Which pinch, which don't, which beat their
    wives with straps.

Go to the Inn on any Friday night

And listen to them while they're getting tight

At the expense of him who stands them
    drinks,

The Mass-Observer with the Hillman Minx.

(Unwitting he of all the knowing winks)

The more he circulates the bitter ales

The longer and the taller grow the tales.

THE DEAR OLD VILLAGE

" Ah ! this is England," thinks he, " rich and
    pure
As tilth and loam and wains and horse-manure,
Slow—yes.   But sociologically sound."
 ' Landlord ! " he cries, " the same again all
    round ! "

The Village Inn

" THE village inn, the dear old inn,
So ancient, clean and free from sin,
True centre of our rural life
Where Hodge sits down beside his wife
And talks of Marx and nuclear fission
With all a rustic's intuition.
Ah, more than church or school or hall,
The village inn's the heart of all."
So spake the brewer's P.R.O.,
A man who really ought to know,
For he is paid for saying so.
And then he kindly gave to me
A lovely coloured booklet free.
'Twas full of prose that sang the praise
Of coaching inns in Georgian days,
Showing how public-houses are
More modern than the motor-car,
More English than the weald or wold
And almost equally as old,
And run for love and not for gold

THE VILLAGE INN

Until I felt a filthy swine
For loathing beer and liking wine,
And rotten to the very core
For thinking village inns a bore,
And village bores more sure to roam
To village inns than stay at home.
And then I thought I *must* be wrong,
So up I rose and went along
To that old village alehouse where
In neon lights is written " Bear ".

Ah, where's the inn that once I knew
    With brick and chalky wall
Up which the knobbly pear-tree grew
    For fear the place would fall ?

Oh, that old pot-house isn't there,
    It wasn't worth our while;
You'll find we have rebuilt " The Bear "
    In Early Georgian style.

But winter jasmine used to cling
    With golden stars a-shine
Where rain and wind would wash and swing
    The crudely painted sign,

81

THE VILLAGE INN

And where's the roof of golden thatch ?
   The chimney-stack of stone ?
The crown-glass panes that used to match
   Each sunset with their own ?

Oh now the walls are red and smart,
   The roof has emerald tiles.
The neon sign's a work of art
   And visible for miles.

The bar inside was papered green,
   The settles grained like oak,
The only light was paraffin,
   The woodfire used to smoke.

And photographs from far and wide
   Were hung around the room :
The hunt, the church, the football side,
   And Kitchener of Khartoum.

THE VILLAGE INN

Our air-conditioned bars are lined
* With washable material,*
The stools are steel, the taste refined,
* Hygienic and ethereal.*

Hurrah, hurrah, for hearts of oak !
* Away with inhibitions !*
For here's a place to sit and soak
* In sanit'ry conditions.*

Station Syren

She sat with a Warwick Deeping,
　Her legs curl'd round in a ring,
Like a beautiful panther sleeping,
　Yet always ready to spring.

Tweed on her well-knit torso,
　Silk on each big strong leg,
An officer's lady—and more so
　Than those who buy off the peg.

More cash than she knew of for spending
　As a Southgate girl at home,
For there's crooning and clinging unending
　For the queen of the girls at the 'drome.

Beautiful brown eyes burning
　Deep on the Deeping page,
Beautiful dark hair learning
　Coiffuring tricks of the age.

STATION SYREN

Negligent hand for holding
   A Flight-Lieutenant at bay,
Petulant lips for scolding
   And kissing the trouble away.

But she isn't exactly partial
   To any of that sort of thing,
So maybe the Air Vice-Marshal
   Will buy her a Bravington ring.

Hunter Trials

It's awf'lly bad luck on Diana,
　　Her ponies have swallowed their bits ;
She fished down their throats with a spanner
　　And frightened them all into fits.

So now she's attempting to borrow.
　　Do lend her some bits, Mummy, *do* ;
I'll lend her my own for to-morrow,
　　But to-day *I*'ll be wanting them too.

Just look at Prunella on Guzzle,
　　The wizardest pony on earth ;
Why doesn't she slacken his muzzle
　　And tighten the breech in his girth ?

I say, Mummy, there's Mrs. Geyser
　　And doesn't she look pretty sick ?
I bet it's because Mona Lisa
　　Was hit on the hock with a brick.

HUNTER TRIALS

Miss Blewitt says Monica threw it,
    But Monica says it was Joan,
And Joan's very thick with Miss Blewitt,
    So Monica's sulking alone.

And Margaret failed in her paces,
    Her withers got tied in a noose,
So her coronets caught in the traces
    And now all her fetlocks are loose.

Oh, it's me now.   I'm terribly nervous.
    I wonder if Smudges will shy.
She's practically certain to swerve as
    Her Pelham is over one eye.

*   *   *   *

Oh wasn't it naughty of Smudges ?
    Oh, Mummy, I'm sick with disgust.
She threw me in front of the Judges,
    And my silly old collarbone's bust.

A Literary Discovery

Sent to the Editor of *Time and Tide*, Dec. 1952

Dear Sir,

I was lately in a second-hand bookshop in East Grinstead and bought for fourpence a green cloth and gilt-edged edition of Longfellow's poems (Crown octavo, Ward Lock & Co., London, 1875). Witness my surprise when I found inside it a piece of yellowish cream-laid paper (water-mark Mudie's Libraries—Swedenborg Bond) with a manuscript poem. There was no surname in the flyleaf of the book, but an inscription read, " To Ellen from her loving husband." The poem was certainly in the same hand as the inscription, a sloping rather clerkly fist suggesting long hours practising pothooks. Seeing that the verses refer to the celebrated novelist Mrs. Henry Wood (1814–1887) whose Christian name was Ellen, I hazard the guess that it is the work of her husband Henry Wood whom she married in 1836. The poem was placed in the leaves where " The Belfry at Bruges " appeared whose famous opening line requires Bruges to be pronounced as two syllables, American style, to obtain full beauty.

In the market-place of Bruges stands the belfry
old and brown.

Not far off is a similar poem " Nüremberg," imparting factual information of a most inspiring kind from the guide-book. I quote a few stanzas from

88

A LITERARY DISCOVERY

" Nüremberg " for it seems to have influenced the
poet of the verses I have found :

In the Courtyard of the castle, bound with many
    an iron band,
Stands the mighty linden planted by Queen
    Cunigunde's hand, . . .

Here, when Art was still religion, with a simple
    reverent heart,
Lived and laboured Albrecht Dürer, the Evan-
    gelist of Art ;

Here Hans Sachs, the cobbler-poet, laureate of
    the gentle craft,
Wisest of the Twelve Wise Masters, in huge
    folios sang and laughed.

I am hoping that some readers, as scholarly as I
am, will be able to throw some light on the verses
that follow. Important questions are raised. Did
the Henry Woods ever live at Gomshall ? When
did Longfellow visit them ? Did Henry Wood sur-
vive his visit ? Was the house renamed ? With
the idea of helping other scholars, I have annotated
the verses. I may say that, if you do not see fit
to print this, I shall send it to *The Times Literary*

7   89

Supplement where it will, no doubt, be published on that interesting back page.

> Where yon crenellated mansion
>
> On the hill surmounts the pines,
>
> Many a long-departed merchant [1]
>
> In the cellar stored his wines,
>
>
> Hock for fish, [2] for pheasant claret,
>
> As the sun sloped slowly down
>
> Over ambient lawns and pinewoods
>
> Backed beyond by Guildford town.
>
>
> Once the railway out of London
>
> Over twenty years ago [3]
>
> To that crenellated mansion
>
> Brought the poet Longfellow.

[1] The Woods then did not build the house but rented or bought it from city friends.

[2] A wine authority tells me that hock with fish is a late innovation.   How late ?

[3] He would have come either to Guildford (L. & S.W.R., L.B. & S.C.R., S.E. & C.R.) or Redhill (S.E. & C.R., L.B. & S.C.R.) and changed on to the beautiful bit of line which runs under Box Hill.   Did he also call on Meredith and Tupper ?   It is a key line (in the poem, I mean, not the railway system) for it helps to date the verses.

A LITERARY DISCOVERY

There were footmen to receive him,
  And a butler, stern as doom
Led him by the beetling antlers [1]
  To the large withdrawing room.

She was waiting to receive him,
  By her side her husband stood
Who alive would see the husband ? [2]
  This was MRS. Henry Wood.

" Mr. Longfellow, delighted
  To receive you in our bowers !
Welcome and a thousand welcomes !
  Rest you here in Gomshall Towers ! " [3]

[1] I do not think this refers to the poet's bushy eye-brows but to the decoration of the hall.
[2] If it is Henry Wood writing, one can well understand the sad implication.
[3] There is no " Gomshall Towers " on the ordnance map to-day. Sheet 170 London S.W. 1 inch. Ordnance Survey Office, Chessington, 1945.

A LITERARY DISCOVERY

Calmly in his Yankee accent

Cultured, carefully and slow

To the greeting of his hostess

Answered Mr. Longfellow :

" Ma'am, your fine historic mansion [1]

Is a dream of mine come true.

'Tis, amid its pines and hemlocks [2]

Some Helvetian rendezvous."

In his ivy-mantled bedroom,

Dirty as he was from town,[3]

'Ere he touched the wash-hand basin [4]

Did he write a poem down.

[1] The poet must be in error.   There is no *old* mansion at Gomshall.   But he may well have thought Gomshall Towers old because of the crenellations, and historic because of its hostess.

[2] The hemlock (*conium maculatum*) is possibly a poetical description for elderberry bushes, which are found in the Gomshall district, and a harbinger or recollection of *Evangeline*.

[3] The word " town " for London was in fashionable use until this century.

[4] There would not, of course, have been running water in the bedroom.   We are to envisage a brass can with a face-towel over it.   The water may have been cold and the poet therefore wrote the poem while waiting for a fresh can to be brought.   We must not lightly accuse him of uncleanliness.

A LITERARY DISCOVERY

" Little Switzerland in England."
    What could please a lady more
Than to find her Surrey mansion
    Had inspired "Excelsior ?"

" Little Switzerland in England "
    Still the name rings in my ears
When around the bend from Gomshall
    Erstwhile Gomshall Towers appears[1],

---

[1] Though the road bends here, I think the railway is intended, for it is more elevated and commands a view of the larger houses.

How to Get On in Society

Originally set as a competition in "Time and Tide"

PHONE for the fish-knives, Norman
   As Cook is a little unnerved ;
You kiddies have crumpled the serviettes
   And I must have things daintily served.

Are the requisites all in the toilet ?
   The frills round the cutlets can wait
Till the girl has replenished the cruets
   And switched on the logs in the grate.

It's ever so close in the lounge dear,
   But the vestibule's comfy for tea
And Howard is out riding on horseback
   So do come and take some with me.

HOW TO GET ON IN SOCIETY

Now here is a fork for your pastries
   And do use the couch for your feet ;
I know what I wanted to ask you—
   Is trifle sufficient for sweet ?

Milk and then just as it comes dear ?
   I'm afraid the preserve's full of stones;
Beg pardon, I'm soiling the doileys
   With afternoon tea-cakes and scones.